[REFUGE]
Meditations for
times of trouble

Simon Donohoe

SOLAS
BOOKS

Written by Simon Donohoe

ISBN: 978-1-7384418-0-8

Layout, cover design and printing by Morse-Brown Design Limited
Published by Solas Books

Acknowledgements

I give thanks to God for many people who have helped to shape and sharpen the pages of this book. In particular, huge thanks go to…

Colin Creighton, who read an early draft of the book. His insightful feedback has made this a more consistent and pastorally sensitive book.

Christopher Ash, whose work on the Psalms has had a huge impact on the way that I read, understand, pray and sing the Psalms. Listening to and reading his teaching has helped me adjust the lens of this book more clearly on Christ.

Ruth Garvey-Williams, whose diligent editing work has made this a more clear and readable book.

John Morse-Brown, who guided me through the unknown waters of publishing. His beautiful design work has made this book look great.

Most of all, Abigail, who has been a constant encouragement, not only through the whole of this project, but for more than ten years of married life has been an immeasurable gift from God. She has helped keep me looking to Christ in both the sunshine and the storms, and helped to make this book better serve real human beings!

Contents

Introduction

"When other helpers fail and comforts flee
Help of the helpless, O abide with me."
(Henry Francis Lyte, Abide with Me)

Some things can only be seen in the brutal winds of the storm.

We spend our lives building shelters. We invest our hopes in DIY refuges to shield us from the gale. We gather money in bank accounts. We place expectations in our relationships. We look after our bodies. We work hard in our job. Yet when the turbulent wind of trouble comes barging into our lives, we see our refuges with new perspective. When the sun is shining, they look like an impenetrable fortress. However, in the swirling gales of hardship the cracks begin to show. Our shelters are exposed as flimsy shacks.

Trouble is an expert at this. I started writing these words on a dark damp winter's day ten months into the Coronavirus pandemic. 2020 left many sitting in the rubble of their refuges. Finances are strained. Jobs are at risk. Families are under pressure. Health is fragile. If it did nothing else, Covid-19 forced us to face up to how unstable our refuges are. They might look good in the sunshine, but when the gusts of trouble begin to blow, we see them for what they really are.

This is a book for those who are battered by the waves of trouble. These words are for those moments when helpers fail and comforts flee. It will not offer quick fixes or clever 'hacks'. They offer little relief in the storm. Instead, I invite you to revisit a fortress where generations before us have found refuge in the face of even the most savage of storms: the words of Psalm 91.

It is not hard to see why this Psalm has been a favourite for generations of believers. This treasury holds some of the sweetest promises in Scripture. At its heart is the offer of refuge. Consider this little book as a tour of the rooms of this fortress. It is an opportunity to savour the deep assurance this Psalm offers, that our souls might find rest in the midst of the whirlwind.

However, Psalm 91 can also be confusing. It sometimes does not seem to line up with our bumped and bruised experience. For example, in verse 10 it promises: *"no evil shall be allowed to befall you, no plague come near your tent"*. Yet, when we are lying in the hospital bed or standing by the graveside, we find it hard to know what to do with a promise like this. Consider this little book like an optician helping us to gaze at Psalm 91 through the right lens. When we read through the lens of Christ, it all comes into focus. These pages offer the opportunity to sing this Psalm *in Christ.*

Above all, that is what Psalm 91 offers us. When the waters of affliction are surging around us, we do not need motivational quotes, 'life hacks' or good advice. What we need most is Jesus. Psalm 91 is woven into the tapestry of Scripture to offer us Christ. He is the impenetrable fortress. When the winds of trouble batter us, and other helpers fail and comforts flee; he is the help of the helpless. He is our refuge.

In the pages to come, you will find 21 short meditations from Psalm 91. They are short: it is hard to focus in the blizzard of trouble. They are meditations: our weary hearts need the promises of God massaged into them if we are to find true rest in the storms.

To help you make the most of these mediations, let me offer two encouragements:

1. Before each chapter **pause, pray and ponder**: Take a moment slowly and prayerfully to read the verse at the start of the chapter (if you have time, consider reading the whole Psalm before each chapter). Ask God to massage his truth into your heart by his Spirit.

2. After each chapter **pause, ponder and pray**: Take a moment to reflect on the verse again. Perhaps write down one thing you want to remember or think of someone you want to share this verse with (one of the most effective ways of working the truth deeper into our own hearts is to share it with others). Then turn that reflection into prayer.

As the winds of trouble churn around us, I invite you to step inside this beautiful psalm with me. Come consider the steadfast beauty of each promise. Come find the rest our weary hearts crave. Come meet the One who is the help of the helpless; our refuge.

Psalm 91 (ESV)

[1] He who dwells in the shelter of the Most High
will abide in the shadow of the Almighty.
[2] I will say to the LORD, "My refuge and my fortress,
my God, in whom I trust."

[3] For he will deliver you from the snare of the fowler
and from the deadly pestilence.
[4] He will cover you with his pinions,
and under his wings you will find refuge;
his faithfulness is a shield and buckler.
[5] You will not fear the terror of the night,
nor the arrow that flies by day,
[6] nor the pestilence that stalks in darkness,
nor the destruction that wastes at noonday.
[7] A thousand may fall at your side,
ten thousand at your right hand,
but it will not come near you.
[8] You will only look with your eyes
and see the recompense of the wicked.

⁹ Because you have made the LORD your dwelling place-
the Most High, who is my refuge-
¹⁰ no evil shall be allowed to befall you,
no plague come near your tent.
¹¹ For he will command his angels concerning you
to guard you in all your ways.
¹² On their hands they will bear you up,
lest you strike your foot against a stone.
¹³ You will tread on the lion and the adder;
the young lion and the serpent you will trample underfoot.

¹⁴ "Because he holds fast to me in love, I will deliver him;
I will protect him, because he knows my name.
¹⁵ When he calls to me, I will answer him;
I will be with him in trouble;
I will rescue him and honour him.
¹⁶ With long life I will satisfy him
and show him my salvation."

Part 1: Approach

The blizzard of trouble can profoundly disorientate us. This loss of perspective can affect how we read Scripture. We rightly run to God's word for comfort when affliction arrives. Yet sometimes we come away with little comfort because of our disorientation. These opening chapters aim to reorientate us. They help us approach this Psalm in such a way that we truly find the refuge we crave as the winds of trouble pound us.

1: The Singer

"Because he holds fast to me in love, I will deliver him;
I will protect him, because he knows my name"
(Psalm 91:14)

When I open the camera app on my smartphone, it offers me two ways of viewing the world. The app opens with a digital version of what I am seeing in front of me: a beautiful sunset, one of my children doing something funny, or that intriguing book on the bookshop shelf. However, with just a tap the camera flips to selfie mode and the screen is filled with a slightly unflattering image of my own face. The view of my pasty face on my screen means I have never fallen in love with 'selfie-mode'. However, the same is not true of my heart.

When trouble comes pounding on my door, I flip my life into 'selfie-mode'. If I am honest, the thoughts that chug around in my mind as I try to sleep are all about me. This trouble has vandalised *my* plans, torn up *my* comfort, and unsettled *my* security. I will turn conversations round to *my woes*, hoping for sympathy and forgetting to be genuinely interested in the person in front of me. I find that the waves of hardship churn up the ugly selfish muck at the bottom of my heart that is easy to hide the rest of the time. If my heart was a smartphone app, it would default to 'selfie-mode'.

In the midst of trouble, it is easy to read the Bible in 'selfie-mode'. When another wave of trouble has knocked me to the sand, and I come to this Psalm thirsty for comfort, it's tempting to read it as if it's all about me. However, if we treat the Bible like this, we actually miss out on the depth of assurance we crave. Only when we recognise that the beautiful promises of this Psalm have not primarily been made to us, will it minister most deeply to our troubled souls. We must allow this Psalm to flip our lens to look outside ourselves.

If we read Psalm 91 in 'selfie-mode' it will discourage us. Take a peek ahead at verse 14: *"Because he holds fast to me in love, I will deliver him."* The gorgeous promises of protection of this Psalm are made to the one who always clings to the LORD in unbreakable loyal love. Let me be honest: Most mornings I do not wake up with a heart swelling with unbreakable loyal love for the Lord. I find many other things jostling in my heart for my affection. I do not instinctively run to the Lord as my refuge. Comfort, reputation, escapism and possessions are all very tempting hiding places. If this is the state of my heart, can I truly claim protection under the shadow of the Almighty? In 'selfie-mode' the potential for discouragement is huge. I will always be left asking myself, "Have I done enough?" "Am I clinging tightly enough?"

Allow the Psalm to flip the camera and look outward. If we do, we see the One who truly holds fast to the LORD in love. We see the One who lived every moment of his days *"in the shelter of the Most High"* (v. 1). We see the One who sings this Psalm in full assurance of the enjoyment of the protective shadow of the Almighty.

This is a song for a king. It is a song for *the* King. Satan recognised this as he quoted this Psalm when tempting

Jesus. He prefaces the quote with *"If you are the Son of God…"* (Matthew 4:3, 6).[1] This picks up God's promises of a king from David's line (see 2 Samuel 7:14; Psalm 2:7). There are many things that Jesus disagrees with Satan about, but he does not disagree on this point. This is a song for the Son of God, the Anointed King.[2]

Jesus is the singer. He enjoys the full assurance of the protective shadow of the Almighty. His resurrection and ascension are proof of this. He has been delivered from every adversity, even death, and now sits securely at the right hand of the Father. He is secure.

As this Psalm flips our camera outward, it offers us something far better than anything 'selfie-mode' could ever provide. It offers us *someone*. As we find ourselves battered by the waves of money troubles or failing health, relational wounds or the unexpected phone call, this Psalm offers us Christ. It offers us the One who is truly secure and truly able to help us in trouble. It fixes our lens on our King, who rests eternally under the protection of the Most High. If our King is secure, then so are we as his people.

So, as we come thirsty for comfort in the midst of our trouble, allow Psalm 91 to flip you out of selfie mode. Start by focusing the lens of your heart on the beauty of the singer, the One who is secure and can truly help. We have someone we can run to as the tide of trouble rises.

---

[1] Christopher Ash, *Psalms For You* (The Good Book Company, 2020), 184.
[2] See Christopher Ash, *Teaching Psalms: Volumes 1 and 2* (Christian Focus, 2017, 2018).

2: The Singers

"For you have died and your life is hidden with Christ in God."
(Colossians 3:3)

Often my first reflex when trouble comes barging through
the door is to hide. Like a child scampering to Mummy and
Daddy's bed in the middle of the night, I look for somewhere to
snuggle into, hoping that trouble will forget about me and move
on. I might take refuge in the distractions of a Netflix box set,
the buzz of an Amazon order, or the solitude of some 'me time'.

When trouble comes, we crave shelter. Yet so many of the hiding
places we run to are flimsy shacks that offer no protection
against the rumbling storms of adversity. Money is fleeting and
soon drains away. Comfort cannot shield us from the harsh
realities of illness. The closest of relationships can let us down.
Even the most faithful of friends simply cannot be with us
constantly and shield us from the storm. Our hiding places
cannot defend us from the onslaught of the storms of trouble.

In the last meditation, we saw that this Psalm is a song for the
King. Jesus is the Singer who enjoys living under the shadow
of the Almighty. He truly clings to the Father in love, and so
enjoys the constant protection of the Most High. He lives in
the solid hiding place. However, this Psalm is not written as a
solo performance. The Singer invites us to join in. He offers us
somewhere to hide.

Perhaps one of the most precious truths of Scripture is this: if
I have trusted Jesus, I am now united to him. Every Christian
believer is one with Christ. He is the head and we, the church,

are his body. A head will never go anywhere without its body. Wonderfully, this means that what is true of him is also true of us. His hiding place is now ours.

If we are one with Christ, we do not need to scrabble desperately for somewhere to hide as the clouds of trouble are forming on the horizon. We do not need to hide because we are already hidden. Here is how the apostle Paul describes our status: *"…you have died and your life is hidden with Christ in God."* (Colossians 3:3). Our life is hidden in Christ. It is eternally secure. No hellish power, no plot of men, and no tempest of tragedy can ever lay a hand on the life we have in Christ.

If we are one with Christ, his death has become our death. We died with him and our guilt no longer stands against us. Therefore, we have nothing to fear when Christ comes to judge. When the storm of God's judgement passes over, we shall be safe, hidden in Christ. The ultimate storm holds no threat to us in Christ.

If we are one with Christ, his resurrection life is our life. We have been raised with him. As he sits secure at the Father's right hand, we are there, spiritually, with him because we are one with him. The storms that rage around us, as painful as they might be, cannot touch our resurrection life. Our true life is hidden secure in Christ, far out of reach of the fiercest waves of trouble.

The reason we run for our hiding places when trouble barges through the door is that we feel threatened. Trouble threatens to take life from us. I started writing this while the Coronavirus pandemic raged across the world. It smashed up our plans, wrenched livelihoods from many hands, and killed thousands. We hid in lockdown in our homes, yet we did not feel any safer. Every shopping trip for essentials and every letter through the door were cracks in our refuge to be exploited by the virus.

However, no pandemic can ever touch our life in Christ. Our life is hidden in Christ. We may die, but death can never sever us from the One who is life. We may lose our income, but no financial crash can plunder the inheritance that can never perish, spoil or fade that is ours in Christ. We may limp through the rest of our earthly days in poor health, but united to Christ, we shall be raised with bodies free from all the effects of the fall.

None of this is to say that we will be magically immune from the pains of this life. Jesus was not. He knew suffering. He knew grief. He knew betrayal. He experienced death. Yes, life may hurt but in Christ none of these things can ultimately harm us. Our life is hidden with Christ under the shadow of the Almighty.

We have a hiding place. As Christ the King sings this from under the shelter of the Most High, we are hidden with him and can join the song. Whatever storms we face, we live our lives under the shadow of the Almighty. We are safe in Christ.

Part 2: Headline (v1-2)

In the mire of hardship concentration levels erode quickly.
In these moments it is hard to focus on the small print.
We need headline truth. The opening verses of Psalm 91 offer
us the psalm at a glance. As we step through the front door of
this Psalm, we are given a succinct orientation to the promise at
its heart: refuge (v. 1). Following this, we are handed a concise
picture of how we can enjoy this promise for ourselves: faith (v. 2).

3: Shadow

"He who dwells in the shelter of the Most High
will abide in the shadow of the Almighty."
(Psalm 91:1)

A few months into a new job and I was sinking. It was not the hard work, I had expected that. Some part of me had invested in this position as my rock to build a future on. When the timbers began to splinter under the weight of expectation, disillusionment began to settle in. I felt exposed. The future felt shaky.

Perhaps you are reading this surrounded by the rubble of your favourite refuge. It is painful to stand in the midst of the crumbling mortar of failing health. It hurts to see the storm beginning to blow through the cracks in the one relationship you thought you could rely on. It is numbing to realise that the last Amazon order has not done anything to strengthen the shaky foundations. At some point the refuges we have run to, or spent years building up around us, will fail. They simply cannot withstand the storms of hardship that a broken world throws at them. When the cracks begin to appear in the stonework, or the masonry begins to tumble, we feel exposed. We feel helpless in the face of the storm.

Why do our refuges fail? They fail because they simply are not strong enough. They snap under the weight of expectation we place on them. Forces far more powerful rage through our broken world. Our health, education, relationships, bank balances, career and comfort are frail fortresses before the onslaught of sin, or the storm of evil, or the tremors of simply living in a broken world.

Psalm 91 is a song to sing in trouble because it offers us the one refuge that cannot be shaken. It offers us a person. The unshakable person. Verse one offers us the Psalm in miniature before we explore the beautiful sights to come: *"He who dwells in the shelter of the Most High will abide in the shadow of the Almighty."*

Pause for a moment. Consider the titles given to God: *He is the Most High.* He sits on the throne, high above every other power. There is no authority like his authority. He takes orders from no one. Every authority that exists, whether visible or invisible, is answerable to him. *He is the Almighty.* He rules in infinite, eternal and unchangeable power. No power in the cosmos can rival his. There are forces in this world that rage beyond our control. They are not beyond his.

The promise at the heart of this Psalm is that the one who makes this God their hiding place will remain under his protection. The authority of the Most High is on their side. The power of the Almighty stands guard over them. Ultimately *"he who dwells"* is referring to only one man. Only one man never gave in to the temptation to find his security anywhere else other than in his Heavenly Father. Only one man is now hidden in the Almighty's hiding place. Jesus now sits in the place of the highest security in the cosmos, secure at the Father's right hand.

Yet for the Christian believer, as we stand in a world of creaking and crumbling refuges, we need not be threatened. If we have entrusted ourselves to Christ, we are hidden in him. He is the head and we, the church, are his body. Reflect on that for a moment: a head never goes anywhere without its body! We are where he is.

In Christ we dwell *"in the shelter of the Most High"*. A 'shelter' is a secret place, a hiding place where the malicious intent of the enemy cannot find us. It is a place of rest. Our true life, our resurrection life will not be discovered and plundered by any power of evil or chaos, it is hidden in safe keeping. We are not promised that suffering or disappointment will never break into our lives. However, in Christ we have the assurance that though they ransack the house, they will never discover nor plunder our true valuables, our eternal life in Christ.

In him, we live under the shadow of the Almighty as members of the family. Under his shadow the fierce blazing heat of the sun cannot harm us. However violently the scorching rays of trouble beat down, we are shielded in his protective shade. We may feel its heat, but it will not sap the life we have in Christ.

We have no need to hide in makeshift shelters as the storm of adversity brews. We are in him. Rest in the refuge you already have as a member of Christ's body. Remind yourself that in Christ the authority of the Most High is on our side and the power of the Almighty stands guard over you. However, strong the winds of adversity blow, *"your life is hidden with Christ in God"* (Colossians 3:3).

4: 'My'

"I will say to the Lord, 'My refuge and my fortress,
my God, in whom I trust.'"
(Psalm 91:2)

One word can change everything. Think about that little word
'my'. A single syllable. Only two letters. Yet it can make all the
difference. That little word has strong hands. It takes hold of
things. It takes something that is 'out there' and brings it 'in
here'. It takes something distant and detached, and makes it
close and connected.

'My' can both be the most ugly and the most beautiful of words.
There is the ugly 'my' of the child snatching at the coveted toy
car or clutching the treasured doll to their breast when Mum
suggests that it might be nice to share. Yet 'my' can also be
capable of the deepest beauty. As the newly married groom
stands up and says "My wife and I..." we know what happens
next. The room erupts in cheers (and a few eyes will shed a tear).
The tender 'my' of a husband and wife draws the other near.

Verse one gives us the headline, the Psalm in miniature. It
summarises all of the beautiful promises to come in the rest of
the Psalm. However, the promise considered in itself is a little
like the vitamin supplements sitting on my kitchen shelf: full of
goodness, but of no benefit to me...until I reach out and ingest
them. Here in this second verse we see the 'my' of faith reaching
out its empty hands to feed on the promises.

Faith sees who God is. He sees the Lord who is a refuge. He
is the place of shelter. Think of a cave: a place of safety from

the howling storm. Think of the cities of refuge in the Old Testament: a place of safety for the person fleeing from those who would take vengeance. He is the shelter from the storms that rage in this fallen world.

He sees the God who is a fortress. He is the place of protection. Think of a mountain stronghold: inside you are high out of reach of the hostile forces. Think of a fortified city, walled and guarded: inside you are protected from the armies outside. He is the place of protection from the hostile forces that stalk this fallen world.

However, for true faith seeing is not enough. Simply seeing the tin of baked beans in the cupboard does me no good. To benefit from it, I must take it inside myself (making sure I open the tin first, of course). Likewise, true faith is not content to simply see who God is. It has a godly hunger to take hold of him as 'mine'. Notice how the singer does not say 'a refuge' but *'my refuge'*; nor does he say 'a fortress' but *'my fortress'*. That is the 'my' of faith.

The voice of verse 2 is the voice of the one singer. Jesus is the ultimate man of faith who says without faltering to the promises of verse 1: "Yes. This is my God and I trust in him." Even as he hung forsaken on the cross, his cries still included the 'my' of faith: *"My God, my God, why have you forsaken me?"* (Mark 15:34). He knew him as his refuge, his fortress. Even through the cross he rested in his shelter and protection.

All of us who have believed in Christ, have been united to him by the Spirit. One with him, all that is his now becomes ours. All that he says 'mine' over he shares with us. His Father is now our Father. In John's gospel, the first words the risen Jesus wanted his disciples to hear were these: *"I am ascending to my Father and your Father, to my God and your God"* (John 20:17). We share in his relationship with the Father. In him, we now join in the song and say to the LORD: *"My refuge and my fortress, my God, in whom I trust"* (Psalm 91:2). In Christ, he is our shelter and protection. We can say these words when the sun shines warmly on us and when the storm howls around us.

One word can change everything. When the storms of adversity rage, 'my' makes all the difference. God is not simply a refuge and a fortress – some powerful God 'out there' somewhere. No, if I am in Christ, he is *my* refuge and *my* fortress. He is present. 'My' makes all the difference.

Part 3: Details (v. 3-13)

Summaries are convenient, but we also need specifics. To know in the abstract that the Lord is my refuge is not enough for our troubled hearts. I need the warm assurance of this refuge to flood the concrete situations of the muck and mess of my life. If v. 1-2 are the headline, v. 3-13 spell out the details. They demonstrate how the promise works out in the tangible experiences of life in this broken world. As we ramble through these details, it allows our troubled hearts to find rest under the shadow of the Almighty in the midst of the multitude of specific troubles we experience.

5: The Poacher and the Plague

"For he will deliver you from the snare of the fowler
and from the deadly pestilence"
(Psalm 91:3)

There have been both moments and seasons in my life when something deep within me has longed that someone might airlift me out of my current situation. Perhaps, you know what that feels like. Your Christian faith has got up the nose of an unbelieving workmate. On the train to work you long to be plucked away from another day of sneers. Your doctor says those words, "I'm afraid it's not good news..." and you long to be anywhere but here.

Whether it is the hostility of human evil or the harmful implications of living in a fallen world, suffering hurts. Somewhere in the midst of the surging emotions is that ache. An ache to be taken away from the pain and away from the hardship.

Verse 3 offers hope for our aching hearts. If verse 1 was the big letters over the entrance gate, with verse 3 we step through the gates into the botanical gardens of this psalm to be intoxicated by the sights and scents of the promises. We are offered true escape.

One of my favourite moments in *the Lord of the Rings* books comes near the end. Unlikely heroes Frodo and Sam lie helplessly surrounded by the fires of Mount Doom, awaiting their impending death. Right before the fires engulf them, the great eagles swoop down and snatch Frodo and Sam in their talons. They are lifted from danger. This is the image of v. 3. The

LORD promises the one who takes refuge in him, *"I will deliver you"*. 'Deliver' literally means to "snatch away".

Notice what the singer of this psalm is snatched away from. First, we meet the *hostile poacher*. Like a vulnerable bird, the singer lives in a world laced with the malicious intent of those who would oppose him. His enemies lay malevolent traps to harm and ensnare him.

The Son of God incarnate was not immune from the fowler's snare. Enemies laid multiple traps for him. A close friend betrayed him. He was ensnared by the chords of death. As his people, we face the same: sneers from workmates, pressure from unbelieving family members, mistreatment in the media, or that friend who no longer walks with you because you hold to the Bible's teaching on the gender issues of our day.

We also live in a broken world polluted by human evil. We are not immune from the callous burglar, the betraying spouse, the drunk driver or the inconsiderate neighbour.

Alongside the poacher is the *harmful plague*. As a result of Adam's sin our world is riddled with disease. Coronavirus, cancer, chronic headaches, typhoid, tummy bugs and tetanus all plague us. Even the simple fact of the pestilence being 'out there' somewhere is enough to disturb us. At the height of the Covid-19 pandemic, even going out to buy some bread and milk was an anxiety-riddled affair.

Scripture does not tell us whether Jesus ever caught the flu (or any other illness). That does not however mean that he is unable to sympathise with us. He truly experienced life in this fallen world. He knew the frailty of a human body. He tasted bodily pain. He wept at the graveside of a beloved friend, a victim of the plague.

In a world infested with poachers and infected with plagues, there is real hope for the one who makes the LORD his refuge. *"He will snatch you away..."* (v.3). Away from the poacher's hostile snares. Away from the noxious plague. Our King has been snatched away. Snatched from the snares of death, he now sits at the Father's side. In his victory, he is untouchable by any poacher. His resurrection body is impervious to any plague.

However, at the same time his body still suffers. He *"is the head of the body, the church"* (Colossians 1:18). One with him, we are his body. We still experience the malice of the poacher and the menace of the plague. Pressure from unbelieving family and painful diagnoses, betrayal by a spouse and heartache at the graveside still afflict us.

Yet we do not suffer without hope. Christ our head has been snatched from danger. No head ever goes anywhere without its body. Where the head goes the body will follow. His present security is our guaranteed future. He has been delivered and soon we will follow. Enemies may lay siege, disease may afflict us, death may grasp hold of us, yet none of them can lay a finger on our future. We shall be snatched away. Away from the hostility and harm of this fallen world. We shall one day follow our exalted head. We shall one day savour resurrection life.

6: Wings

"He will cover you with his pinions,
and under his wings you will find refuge;
his faithfulness is a shield and buckler."
(Psalm 91:4)

There are seasons when the murky clouds cluster and the squall of trouble breaks over us. Perhaps one of the things I find hardest in these moments is the sense of being exposed. Affliction exposes our vulnerability. Every shape of trouble has this effect: the dwindling bank account, the doctor's diagnosis, the relational mess, the wayward child, the road accident, the hostile workmates; they all expose our vulnerability.

It is in these seasons, that I realise I am not as emotionally resilient as I thought. I really am quite defenceless against the forces of chaos that tear through this fallen world. I feel like a young chick in a rainstorm or a naked soldier in the middle of violent conflict.

Here, in verse 4, is reassurance for the vulnerable. The previous verse offered protection from poacher and plague. Now we hear of the nature of that protection. The Lord is all the protection we need. In him, both tender strength and powerful compassion come together. Two very different images of protection are united in him: the motherly wings and the military shield.

There is tenderness in his protection. It is the warmth of the mother hen's wings. *"He will cover you with his pinions, and under his wings you will find refuge"* (v. 4). Think of the mother hen as the first gusts of the storm flutter her feathers. In tenderness, she gathers her chicks under her wings. They are close. They are covered. She is their shelter, a refuge from the wind.

This image takes us to the heart of the covenant. Over the ark of the covenant in the Holy of Holies were the overshadowing wings of the cherubim. The tender protection promised here is the protection offered by the covenant, sealed in the blood of the covenant.[3]

Jesus sung this Psalm in the assurance of his Father's tender protection. He rested in the protection of the covenant promises, a rest that enabled him to sleep even in the midst of the raging storm. He offers this tender protection to others. Lamenting over Jerusalem, he says *"How often would I have gathered your children together as a hen gathers her brood under her wings, and you were not willing!"* (Matthew 23:37). His heart gushes with compassion, offering tender covenant protection to all who will take refuge under his wings.

Alongside this tenderness there is toughness. It is the strength of the unyielding shield. His *"faithfulness is a shield and buckler"* (v.4). There is unyielding protection in the Lord's covenant faithfulness. The promises guaranteed by the blood of the covenant are a shield, preserving us from the piercing arrow. They are a bulwark, covering us on all sides with protection.

Jesus sung this Psalm in the assurance of the tough protection of the covenant promises. No hostile arrow could ultimately harm him. He offers this tough protection to others. If we are

---

[3] Christopher Ash, *Psalms For You* (The Good Book Company, 2020), 182.

found in him, he surrounds us on all sides. His faithfulness is unyielding. No arrow that flies in this fallen world will ever pierce through the promises that are 'yes' and 'amen' in him.

Life frequently exposes our vulnerability. An unexpected cancer diagnosis or unforeseen expenses and I feel like a newly hatched chick in a thunderstorm. Antagonism in work or betrayal by a loved one and I'm like a soldier naked in the heat of the battle. I am weak. I am fragile. I might cover it convincingly at times, but the storm of trouble quickly tears off my coverings. Instead of chasing after my coverings as they're tossed by the winds of affliction, I must look to Christ. In him alone, I find the tender and tough protection that shelters me through the storm.

What beautiful qualities come together in Christ! He tends his sheep in tenderness and surrounds them with toughness. The radiant beauty of these qualities come into sharper focus when we realise what the mother hen's wings and the soldiers shield have in common: substitution. When the storm breaks the mother hen tenderly enfolds her vulnerable chicks under her wings to protect them. In order to give them refuge, she must be battered by the wind and rain. As the arrow flies in the heat of battle, the tough shield must be pierced in order to keep the soldier safe.

In your vulnerability, keep looking to the cross. Christ was battered by the storm of divine wrath and pierced by the arrow of judgment. Therefore, the ultimate storm of God's just anger at sin will not touch us if we are found in him. The tender wings and tough shield of covenant protection are guaranteed by his pierced side.

7: Night and Day

"You will not fear the terror of the night,
nor the arrow that flies by day..."
(Psalm 91:5)

Night time can be hard. I have always found it hard to sleep.
I tend to over-think things, especially when my head is on
the pillow. Somehow in the silent darkness, everything seems
worse. Fears clamber into our minds and play around. The
'what if' monster terrorises us over money pressures, family
concerns or health worries. Threats feel more sinister as we
analyse the workplace hostility, marital disagreement or
opposition to the gospel.

Yet daytime can be equally hard. Perhaps sleep has been an
escape. Waking brings the realisation that trouble has not gone
away. We must face that conversation in work, the doctor's
appointment or the ongoing mess of that relationship.

The one who makes the Lord his refuge has been promised
protection. Protection under the wings of the covenant God.
Verse 5 now shows us the implication: *"You will not fear"*.
Whether it is the terror of night or the threats of the day *"you
will not fear"*.

We need not fear the terror of the night. Under his wings we have
refuge from everything that stalks in the darkness. Things can
be more frightening in the night. Loneliness can become a
suffocating monster in the night watches. Fears forgotten in the
activities of the day, return to haunt us. On the sleepless pillow,

hope can drain from the ongoing situation with our health, marriage or finances.

We are not told exactly what 'the terror of the night' is. Perhaps, that is the point. The unknown and unseen terrifies us. There are possible demonic overtones here.[4] There are invisible forces of evil and chaos that terrorise our world, and they are not idle. If we are honest, it is frightening.

There is assurance through the night. We need not fear these terrors. We are never promised that we will not face them. However, sheltered under his wings, none of the terrors of night can ultimately harm us. The Lord's protection does not turn in for the night. We need not fear.

We need not fear the arrow that flies by day. Behind the shield of his faithfulness, we have refuge from the dangers of the daytime. When daytime comes, we are forced to confront the fears we temporarily escaped in sleep. Sometimes a new morning feels like getting kitted out for battle. We go into the day with trepidation, fearful of what arrows will fly at us today. A new day ushers us into the battlefield of chronic headaches, family pressure, marital struggles, mental illness, or antagonism for belonging to Christ.

There is assurance through the day. We need not fear these dangers. We are told the arrows will surely fly. However, protected by his shield, none can truly pierce us. His protection does not evaporate with the morning dew. We need not fear.

———————

[4] Christopher Ash, *Psalms For You* (The Good Book Company, 2020), 182.

Christ walked without fear by night and day. He faced the terrors of night: He was often awake through the watches of the night. He was arrested in the darkness of Gethsemane, and unjustly tried through the night. He faced the arrows by day: There were the attempts to stone him, or throw him off the cliff. Through all this, he walked without fear. Night and day, he stood under the protection of the Most High.

Our life is hidden in him. His fearlessness is ours. Through the watches of the night, whatever terrors may skulk about, we are hidden under his wings. Through the battlefield of the day, whatever arrows may whizz through the air, we are covered by his shield.

However, the reality is that I do not often feel fearless. Many times, I feel afraid. We need to assure ourselves that his protecting cover does not depend on how fearless we feel. His objective shelter does not ebb and flow with our subjective feelings. Our hope is in the One who never feared, who always walked in perfect trust. We are hidden in him. Even at our moments of greatest fear, if we are in him, we are as safe as if we were in glory already.

It may be that the night is the worst for you. The 'what if' monster clambers into your mind for another sleepless night. It may be mornings that are hardest. Fresh fears awake as you head out to the battlefield of another day. Take comfort: day or night, you are covered in Christ. None of the fears of day or night can touch our life in him.

8: Darkness and Fierce Light

"You will not fear...
the pestilence that stalks in darkness,
nor the destruction that wastes at noonday."
(Psalm 91:6)

When do you feel most insecure? When does safety feel furthest from you?

Sometimes it is in the shadows of darkness. In the dark, it is hard to see. Threats stalk unseen in the shadows. The familiar footpath home is more uncertain in the gloom of the winter evening. Anxieties feel more sinister on the pillow in the blackness of night.

Sometimes it is in the fierce midday light. In the scorching glare of noon, we are exposed. The cancer diagnosis, the betrayal, or being made redundant can be more terrifying when their devastating effects are seen in daylight.

Whether we are shuddering in the enveloping dark or trembling in the glaring light, the truth of verse 6 is tonic for our palpitating hearts. The imagery of verse 5 intensifies in verse 6. Night becomes deep darkness, day gives way to fierce midday light. Yet, with heightened threats comes deeper comfort. We need not fear. The one who makes the Lord their refuge is shielded at all times from all threats.

In him we are sheltered from the pestilence that stalks in darkness. This is an intense blackness. In the murky shadows lurks the unseen threat, the invisible enemy. Viruses, like Covid-19 or

Ebola or Dengue fever, evoke so much fear because they stalk unseen. Cancer is no different. The far more sinister pandemic, the cancer of sin that plagues every human heart, also does its work unseen.

The words of verse 6 have echoes of the demonic. There are invisible forces of evil at work in this world. Temptations that slither unseen into our day. Satan whispers lies to our hearts. Loved ones silently hardened by sins deceitfulness.

In the darkness, remember this: you need not fear. The shelter of the Most High does not fade with the dimming light. The pestilence may stalk us, but our eternity is safe under the Almighty's shadow.

In him we are sheltered from the destruction that wastes at noonday. This is the scorching of fierce light. It is the searing heat of the desert sun. The destruction does not need the aid of shadows to sow fear into hearts. The terror of the tsunami or the car accident, the horror of the terrorist attack or the house fire are ghastly in the daylight.

The forces of evil also leave devastation behind. Recently, a friend and fellow pastor walked out on his wife and young child, left his ministry and dropped off the radar. The devastation he left behind is beyond counting. It is no different with abuse, marital infidelity, or deceit. Sin is a vandal.

In the searing heat, remember this: even in the devastating pain, you need not fear. The destructive forces of evil may leave parts of our lives in rubble. However, it cannot touch the life we have in Christ.

Jesus rested in this confidence. He was stalked in the blackness. At the prompting of Satan, Judas slipped out into the night to betray him. In the darkness of Gethsemane, he wrestled with temptation. He was besieged at noonday. Under the baking desert sun, he was assaulted by the devil's lies. Repeated plots were made to rupture his mission. Yet he walked without fear.

However storm-tossed you feel, your true life is hidden securely in Christ. The sinister forces of darkest night and fiercest noon cannot harm us if we are in him. Surely, then no other force can ultimately harm us. We are secure.

The images of verses 5-6 are terrifying. However, they are not there to panic us but to soothe our troubled hearts. These threats may be hideous, but under the wings of the Almighty our true life is safe. Our life in Christ is protected at all times from even the darkest of threats. Whether you are being stalked in the shadows of darkness, or you sit in the rubble of the noonday devastation, know this: you are secure in Christ. Ultimately, we need not fear.

9: Standing

"A thousand may fall at your side,
ten thousand at your right hand,
but it will not come near you."
(Psalm 91:7)

Hardship is a disorientating blizzard. It is hard to keep perspective in the turbulence of the blizzard. The trouble I am currently facing seems to overshadow everything. Recently I developed tinnitus. All I could think about for the first few days was the constant ringing in my ears. It did its best to say to me: "I'm your biggest problem".

Suffering steals our perspective. It is hard to see beyond the chronic fatigue, the unpaid bills or the family feud. Like driving in a snowstorm, our afflictions obscure our windscreen, doing all they can to convince us they are *the* big problem.

In this disorienting blizzard, the Bible offers us the perspective we so desperately need. It enables us to see through the storm that our problem is soberingly deeper than any of the afflictions that buffet us. Yet it also lifts us above the storm to see the solution is gloriously complete and unshaken by any of our afflictions.

In verses 5-6, we met the darkest threats of night and the most devastating forces of the day. However, in verses 7-8 we are introduced to the most dangerous threat. We meet the extremity of danger. Without warm up we are ushered into the gruesome core of a bloody battle. We are forced to watch soldiers being cut down all around us. Yet, this is not a portrait of any mere battle.

This is a preview of the final battle. Verse 8 announces this as *"the recompense of the wicked"*. This is God's judgement being poured out on human sin.

I am plucked out of mulling over my tinnitus to be reminded that my biggest problem is the wrath of God. Cancer is horrendous, betrayal is agonising, depression is harrowing, and I cannot for a moment minimise them. However, in light of the judgement to come they are cut down to size. If I face an eternity shut out from the goodness of God, how much will it matter if the chemotherapy was successful? Our problem is deeper than the blizzard in the windscreen.

However, we are not left in the depths of despair. The promise of verse 7 is glorious. On that day of judgement a *"thousand may fall at your side, ten thousand at your right hand, but it will not come near you"*. The person who has made the Lord their refuge shall stand. They shall be untouched by the blaze of God's righteous anger against sin. They stand in a right relationship with God.

Who shall stand? Ultimately, it's Christ. He is the true man. He truly made the Lord his fortress. He shall stand. In fact, he'll be the judge on that day. His resurrection proves it. But what about us? Our future depends on our relationship to Jesus. If we are one with him, we are joined to him as a body to its head. Augustine, the early church father, said as he pondered this verse: "Were these words addressed to the Head alone?

Surely not"[5]. As Christ's body, we cannot be separated from the blessings enjoyed by our head.

On earth, our head did not insist on his right to this promise. At the cross, he fell under judgment as all around him stood in mockery. Because he fell, we shall stand. In him, we stand in the place where the fire of God's wrath has already burnt. Fire will not burn the same place twice. In him, we shall be untouched by the blaze on that day.

Trouble is claustrophobic. It obscures our windscreen and steals our perspective. Whatever blizzard you find yourself blinded by, let verse 7 restore your perspective. My problem is far deeper than any wounds I will face in this life. Yet, this, the deepest of all my problems, has already been dealt with fully at the cross. My future is guaranteed. This gives us hope in the whirlwind.

The hardship you face at the moment may seem to dictate your life, but it does not ultimately define you. The affliction you face may drag on for years, but it does not ultimately write your destiny. Your suffering may seem to rob you of a future, but it cannot steal your ultimate security.

In the midst of the tears, remember this: in Christ you shall stand. On that day of the final battle others may fall around you, but you shall stand. You are not destined for wrath but for glory. May the warmth of this sunshine melt the blinding snow from your windscreen.

---

[5] Augustine, 'Expositions on the Book of Psalms' in Philip Schaff (ed), *The Complete Ante-Nicene & Nicene and Post Nicene Fathers Collection* Kindle Edition (Catholic Way, 2014), location 334856.

10: Look

*"You will only look with your eyes
and see the recompense of the wicked."*
(Psalm 91:8)

Not all of our afflictions are impersonal. Some troubles have a human face. It might be the workplace bully, the drunk driver, the unfaithful spouse, the venomous liar or the unexpected mugger. Sometimes our suffering is the result of human evil. Often this is the most painful form of suffering.

Being the recipient of another's wrong rouses an aching in us. We long for wrong to be put right. We hunger for justice to be done. If we are not careful this longing can turn sour. I fantasise about vengeance. My imagination repeatedly concocts scenarios in which I am ladling out revenge. The way I speak about that person takes on a new sharpness. In different ways, we attempt to bring ourselves justice. Yet, our efforts never establish that sense of rightness, so we feel either hopeless or bitter. Left unsupervised, this longing can grow into a burden that either wearies or embitters our hearts.

Verse 8 offers rest. It snaps the cords, allowing the burdens to drop from our hearts. It whispers to our longing hearts, "There's no need to strive". Verse 7 transported us vividly into the middle of the final battle, the moment God's wrath on sin is poured out. Verse 8 now announces the good news to our aching hearts: justice shall be done.

If we are hidden in Christ, an hour is coming when we shall *"see the recompense of the wicked"* (v. 8). Evil shall be repaid.

No moral muck will be swept under the carpet of the cosmos. No culprit will be left 'at large'. When we scream inwardly in our pain, crying out for something to be done about the devastating hit and run or the damage caused by years of abuse or lies, we know we will not yearn forever. When we struggle against that swelling bitterness over the incessant bullying on the building site or that moment of betrayal, we are assured we will not wrestle forever.

The balm of this verse soothes all the more deeply when we notice that the only contribution required of us is simply to behold: *"You will only look with your eyes"* (v.8). No audience participation is required. Justice is in his hands. It has been taken out of ours. The Lord shall establish justice on behalf of his abused people. All we will do is look on.

Jesus rested in this promise. No-one experienced more injustice than he. The One true man, alone free from any stain of sin, was conspired against, despised and rejected, betrayed and arrested, condemned with false charges, ridiculed and crucified. Yet, as he was bombarded with wrongs, not once did he take vengeance into his own hands. Instead he trusted his Father's promise: *"When he was reviled, he did not revile in return; when he suffered, he did not threaten, but continued entrusting himself to him who judges justly"* (1 Peter 2:23).

He has now been vindicated. On the third day, he was raised from the clutches of the grave and declared to be the judge. He shall bring about final justice and he is perfectly qualified to do so. Free from personal vendettas, he will judge with perfect justice. He shall come to act on behalf of his wronged people.

Here is cool water for our thirsty hearts: justice is coming. Justice was accomplished for us in the past as he bore our condemnation at the cross. That final day holds no terror for those who are in Christ. Justice will be accomplished for us as he comes to vindicate his people.

Here is rest for our burdened hearts. I do not need to be the judge. I can lay down that burden. I can place that hunger for wrongs to be righted into Christ's hands. I no longer need to fantasise about vengeance for the drunk driver or the controlling spouse. Vengeance is the Lord's. He's got this sorted. I can soften my tone with my abusive co-worker or the betraying friend. The Lord will call her to account. My imagination can rest from concocting vengeful scenarios. He has judgement planned. Justice is in his hands. It has been taken out of mine. Here is a balm for bitter hearts. Here is rest for weary souls. We will not ache for justice forever.

It is painful to be the recipient of another's evil. It is excruciating at times. Yet, in our sorrows we can look forward with hope for the hour our King establishes impeccable justice. All we will do on that day is look. He has got this.

11: No Exceptions

"Because you have made the LORD your dwelling place–
the Most High, who is my refuge–
no evil shall be allowed to befall you,
no plague come near your tent."
(Psalm 91:9-10)

Sometimes, as we wearily clutch onto hope in the midst of
the gales of trouble, the lie is hissed into our ear: "This is the
exception. This particular trouble you are going through…
it is the exception." The subtle voice insinuates that the small
print of the promises do not cover *this kind* of chronic pain, *this*
leukaemia, *this* situation of marital mess, or *this form* of subtle
bullying. We are unsettled. We fear the promises we placed our
feet on, might turn out to like the car insurance we bought a
couple of years back, not quite as 'comprehensive' as advertised.
Is the trouble battering me really covered by the promise?

Verses 9-10 come with reassuring comprehensiveness. They
gather the themes of the psalm so far and rub them more deeply
into our hearts. If you have made your home in the Lord (v.9)
comprehensive assurance is yours. The One who has been the
dwelling place of his people in all generations is our home
(Psalm 90:1-2).

He is our home. Our home is impregnable, comprehensively
invulnerable. No exceptions. Hidden in Christ *"no evil shall be
allowed to befall you"* (v. 10). The malicious forces of evil will not
sink their claws into us. Hidden in him *"no plague [shall] come
near your tent"* (v. 10). No threat will pierce the canvas of our
fragile humanity.

When troubles gatecrash our lives, they expose our weakness. We are not as resilient as we assumed. Faced with the chaotic storm, I am more like a tent than a stone castle: vulnerable, easily torn and so easily broken. Yet, in Christ, the tent of our human frailty rests within the solid walls of the eternal God, protected from every evil and guarded from every plague. The promise comes with comprehensive cover.

But wait… These words seem to jar against my experience of life in this world. These words do not feel grounded in reality. We are told *'no evil shall befall you'*… but what about the corrupt police officer, the abusive ex or the over demanding Dad? We are assured *'no plague shall come near your tent'*… but what about the cancer diagnosis, the debilitating medical bills or chronic migraines?

One of Satan's strategies for sabotaging faith is to sever the melody of this promise from the whole symphony of Scripture. He wants me to assume that, if I am a believer, nothing bad will ever happen to me. He knows that if I am convinced of that, I will turn from the Lord when trouble inevitably visits me.

However, the sublime melody of this promise can only be heard when woven into its place in Scripture's grand symphony. When we listen to the whole symphony, and not just isolated notes, we find we are not alone. Jesus knows our experience. He experienced the claws of evil and the lashes of plague with a depth we never will. It is not without reason Isaiah called him the Man of Sorrows.

As Christ prepared his disciples to suffer, he promised them: *"You will be delivered up even by parents and brothers and relatives and friends, and some of you they will put to death. You will be hated by all for my name's sake. But not a hair of your head will perish."* (Luke 21:18).

You will be put to death…but not a hair of your head will perish. How does that work? If my true life is hidden with Christ in God, nothing can touch it. We may face hellish evil in this life but on resurrection morning, we will rise unharmed. We may be sorely afflicted by plague but on resurrection morning, we shall awake unscathed. We may lose everything in this life but on resurrection morning, we will enjoy our rust and robber-proof eternal inheritance.

If you are one with Christ, you are as secure as he is. He is our home and our home is impenetrable. However malicious the evil or noxious the plague, they cannot make even the slightest scratch on our eternal future. Hidden in Christ, nothing that afflicts us in this fallen world, however painful, can imperil our resurrection hope. We shall rise on resurrection morning to a world where every tear is wiped away, and sorrow and suffering, pain and pandemics are forever in the past. No exceptions.

12: Refuge

"the Most High, who is my refuge"
(Psalm 91:9b)

I have a loaf of bread in my kitchen cupboard. I need it… but it is currently useless to me. I need food to sustain my body. However, simply being in possession of a loaf of bread and keeping it safe in my cupboard will not nourish me. I need to open the door, cut myself a slice and eat it.

The Psalmist has been stocking up with the richest of promises. They are spiritually nourishing and delectable. However, he knows it is not enough to have promises in the cupboard. They are there to be fed on. In verse 9, he interrupts himself mid-sentence to take a bite of the promise: *"the Most High, who is my refuge"*. That little word 'my' appears again. It is the 'my' of faith and it comes with teeth to feed on the promise.

In the tumult and turmoil of the tempest, what we need most is to feed. Our weary souls need the nourishment of the promises of God. This will mean consciously bringing the God of the promise to mind and resting in him.

The Most High is my refuge.

When faced with the malicious intent of the fowler's snare: cold shoulders in the neighbourhood, betrayal by someone I trusted, pressure from unbelieving family…

The Most High is my refuge.

When threatened by the virulent threat of the deadly pestilence:

crippling pain, debilitating chemotherapy, chronic headaches, Cystic fibrosis…

The Most High is my refuge.

When fear swells as the terror of the night invades my thoughts: suffocating loneliness, haunting anxieties, depression's blackness, unseen forces, memories of abuse…

The Most High is my refuge.

When anxiety rises over the arrow that flies by day: awakening to unchanged circumstances, unrelenting marital struggles, unmet debts, ongoing abuse…

The Most High is my refuge.

When the pestilence stalks me in the darkness: the unseen threat, the invisible enemy, the cancer of sin, the ongoing darkness that lurks in my heart…

The Most High is my refuge.

When frozen before the horror of the destruction that wastes at noonday: the life-shattering phone call, the sobering news report, the unforeseen accident…

The Most High is my refuge.

When others fall around us and we fear we are next: when someone we thought was a believer walks away from the faith, when the misconduct of a trusted leader is revealed…

The Most High is my refuge.

Christ is my refuge.

13: Guards

*"For he will command his angels concerning you
to guard you in all your ways."*
(Psalm 91:11)

Vulnerability is a lonely feeling.

Our fragile little family feels the pressure of a culture
increasingly hostile to the gospel. Anxiety swells as we send our
children off to school, where they face a hostile squeeze for their
faith, not only from peers, but now also from teaching staff. The
swirling secular forces are too strong for our little family. We feel
vulnerably alone.

Our fragile little church feels the pressure of a hostile culture.
Concerns grow over the viability of our evangelistic efforts as the
gush of social media posts reveal that we are no longer viewed
as irrelevant, but now dangerous. These blazing secular forces are
too strong for our little church. We feel vulnerably alone.

In the unrelenting slog against sin, in the furnace of adversity, in
the frustrations of a fractured world, we feel vulnerably alone.

Who is on our side?

Verse 11 announces that vulnerable loneliness is met by the
protective presence of heaven's armies. The reason the one who
has made the Lord their refuge can know security (v. 9-10) is
that they stand under the personal protection of the Almighty's
armies (v. 11).

The orders come from the top: *"he will command his angels concerning you"* (v. 11). The orders are comprehensive: *"to guard you in all your ways"* (v. 11). In the first rays of a summer's morning or the soggy gloom of a winter's night, resting on the familiar mattress or struggling with unfamiliar struggles, the one who has made the Lord their refuge is attended incessantly by heavens bodyguards. Once, the Lord opened the eyes of a young servant boy, troubled by besieging enemies, to see the heartening sight of the flaming hosts of heavens forces filling the surrounding mountains (2 Kings 6:8-17). In the same way, this verse gives us spiritual goggles to see the reassuring presence of God's protection.

However, before we seize this promise, we must understand that it was addressed to God's chosen King. It offers the king the protection he needs for his God-given task. Jesus was tempted by Satan to abuse the promise and wave it around like a lucky charm without trusting the God of the promise.[6] On the pinnacle of the temple Satan whispered, *"If you are the Son of God, throw yourself down"* (Matthew 4:6) as he quoted v. 11-12. Yet, Jesus did not need to jump to prove he is the Son who enjoys heaven's protection. After resisting Satan's enticements, *"angels came and were ministering to him"* (Matthew 4:11). Later, at the empty tomb, it was angels who stood guard. One day, he shall come in glory and *"all the angels with him"* (Matthew 25:31).

However, when Peter swung his sword to prevent Jesus' arrest, he did not take advantage of this privilege: *"Do you think that I*

---

[6] Christopher Ash, *Psalms For You* (The Good Book Company, 2020), 184.

cannot appeal to my Father, and he will at once send me more than twelve legions of angels" (Matthew 26:53). Jesus went to the cross so that we might share this promise with him. One with him, we share in the protection of the king's royal bodyguards. Heavens armies are now *"sent out to serve for the sake of those who are to inherit salvation"* (Hebrews 1:14).

Vulnerability is a lonely feeling.

The howling seas of cultural hostility are a lonely place for my little family to sail. The intensifying temperature of society's pressure to conform is an isolating place for our little church to live. The relentless slog against sin, the bewildering pain of adversity, the unending frustrations of a fallen world, are lonely places to live out our lives as God's people. Yet, if we were given goggles to see spiritual realities, the mountains around us would be glinting with the innumerable ranks of heaven's armies. If we are Christ's, he has placed us under the protection of his royal bodyguards. They stand by at his command to ensure every one of his flock make it to their inheritance.

In him we are not alone. Heaven's hosts are on our side.

14: Held

"On their hands they will bear you up,
lest you strike your foot against a stone."
(Psalm 91:12)

In the midst of a season wrestling with the symptoms of depression, an increasing weight seemed to be pressing upon me. I felt emptied of any strength to carry myself to the end of the day. The weeks that splayed ahead of me felt fatiguingly impossible. I felt burdened beyond my strength. The relentless darkness of depression seems to suck all strength from our souls.

The daily slog against sin can have the same effect. The struggle to subdue the dragon of sinful anger from erupting again is a burden too heavy to bear. The fight to treasure Christ above the sparkling lures of the shop windows or the Amazon basket can drain our soul's vigour. The pressures of opposition can burden us beyond our strength. The unrelenting drip of snide comments from an unbelieving spouse, or the subtle pressure from those with power in our denomination to conform to our culture can sap our spiritual stamina.

Living for Christ in a broken world often leaves us weak and weary. The promise of v.11-12 assure us that in the Lord, we are not left submerged when burdened beyond our strength. Satan delights to wield this promise as a temptation to arrogance (Matthew 4:6). Yet for those who cling in humble dependence to the covenant God, this promise is a well of deep refreshment.

Our weakness is met with the Lord's tenderness. His people do not need to be strong because they are held by the One who is.

He has commanded his invisible army to carry his weary saints: *"On their hands they will bear you up"* (v. 12).

The picture is something like this: Walking to the local shop is a very different experience for my one-year-old son than it is for me. A two minute stroll for me is an exhausting hike for him. A tame trip for me, is for him a journey littered with perils. For him, to meet the neighbour's dog is to be confronted with a beast the size of a hippo. When his legs get weary and he plonks himself down on the pavement, or when the dog next door comes patrolling his patch, I hoist my vulnerable son into my arms. In Christ, the Most High God is our Father who looks on us in gentle compassion. He tenderly carries his children and employs the might of heavens armies to do so. With a bit of a Victorian flavour, Charles Spurgeon describes the picture of v.12: "as nurses carry little children, with careful care, so shall these glorious spirits upbear each individual believer" [7]

Christ was not ashamed to make this promise his own. In becoming flesh, the one who is God truly experienced the weakness and weariness of human life. After 40 days without sustenance, followed by the lashes of Satan's tempting, he was tenderly ministered to by angels (Matthew 4:11). Since we are one with him, he shares with us the tender care offered here. In Christ, we are gripped in the gentle strength of the Lord who carries his people.

When the darkness of depression has drained all stamina from our soul, it is his strength that carries us and keeps us in Christ.

---

[7] Charles Spurgeon, *The Treasury of David: Volume 2* (Hendrickson, 2008), 93.

When the dragon of sinful anger seems untameable, it is his might that keeps us in the battle. When the opposition seems about to strangle us, it is his hand that keeps us keeping on.

This is not just a promise for the big events. It is for the little moments also: *"lest you strike your foot against a stone"*. The most significant battles are fought in the little moments: modelling Christ's gentleness when the kids have gone beyond cranky, keeping on praying when the fog of depression will not dissipate, trusting Christ in the stress of unrealistic expectations at work, showing patient love when slapped by another snide remark from an unbelieving sibling. In the little moments, we are held in his tender grip.

When burdened beyond your strength, remember the tender hands of the Almighty. At times, we might feel like a toddler trying to navigate the tussles of a city centre Main Street. Remember the compassionate arms of our Father in heaven. Usually we will only see this in retrospect. After over two years scuffling off-and-on with symptoms of depression, I said to my wife in a moment of melancholy: "I feel like I cannot make it through another week." Her response: "You said that before… over two years ago".

He carries his children.

15: Crushed

"You will tread on the lion and the adder;
the young lion and the serpent you will trample underfoot."
(Psalm 91:13)

When I came to Christ, I did not develop immunity to being affected by the evils that contaminate this world. Neither did you. We are still exposed to the malice of playground taunts, the bitterness of subtle undermining by a co-worker, the brutality of the phone scammer, the malevolence of marital unfaithfulness.

If we could peek behind the curtains of the cosmos, we would see that a far more sinister evil lurks behind the atrocities that blight our world. We have a malicious enemy. He skulks ferociously: *"Your adversary the devil prowls around like a roaring lion, seeking someone to devour"* (1 Peter 5:8). Satan is sly and poisonous: *"the serpent was more crafty than any other beast of the field that the LORD God had made"* (Genesis 3:1). He revels in showing subtle and ferocious hostility towards the people of God.

Life is a battle, and it often feels like we are being trounced. We collapse frustrated into bed, disheartened in the slog against sin. The allure of iniquity seemed to overpower us again today. We anxiously wonder what future God's people have in our land as the swelling forces of 'political correctness' threaten to clamp jaws on the Church. That prowling lion and venomous serpent appears to be winning.

Verses 11-12 offered security. Verse 13 promises victory. The King shall trample on ferocious lions and cunning serpents. However, this is not simply the ability to duff up a couple of wild animals. Hear the echoes of the promised triumph God's people have longed for: *"The LORD God said to the serpent...'I will put enmity between you and the woman, and between your offspring and her offspring; he shall bruise your head, and you shall bruise his heel'"* (Genesis 3:14-15). This is victory, not over a serpent, but over the serpent. This is triumph, not over *a* lion, but over *the* foe who prowls like one.

This King is the Serpent Crusher. Creation has been aching for him since Adam's teeth sunk into the unauthorised fruit. He dealt our ancient serpentine enemy his death blow as he hung on the cross. He is coming in beautiful glory to throw down that poisonous dragon, never again to trouble his people. *This King is the Lion from Judah's tribe.* He has conquered (Revelation 5:5). Satan may prowl like a lion, but he is an imposter. Christ shall one day roar in the majestic ferocity of final judgment. He has the last word. No force can imperil his triumph over evil.[8]

With stunning wonder, we hear the apostle Paul pluck this language and administer it to ordinary believers. To common garden Christians, who struggle through the muck, mess and mayhem of life, he says: *"The God of peace will soon crush Satan under your feet"* (Romans 16:20). Under my feet?! How is this possible? I am faulty, flawed and feeble. I flinch at the slightest whiff of antagonism. I am overwhelmed in the slog against sin. How could I ever triumph?

We triumph by faith: *"this is the victory that has overcome the world – our faith"* (1 John 5:4). My faith fuses me to the Serpent

---

[8] Christopher Ash, *Psalms For You* (The Good Book Company, 2020), 183.

Crusher, the Lion from Judah's tribe, and he shall overcome. It is not that there is any inherent power in my faith. The power is in the One my faith rests in, and he will tread on the lion and trample the serpent. His victory is inevitable.

As we await that day, we will be pounded by Satan's subtle ferocity and fierce subtlety. We will be bruised by the unrelenting battle with the remnants of the tumour of sin in our hearts. We will feel the daily drip drip of serpentine enticements to sin. Our children will face the malice of the playground taunts. We will be cut by the sneers of neighbours on our estate. The squeezing social pressures of a secular world will threaten to crush us. The malevolence of marital unfaithfulness will continue to vandalise our churches. Bulging pride will continue to batter the culture of love our church families seek to nurture. In this world, we are not immune from the brutality of evil.

Yet, though we weep, though we hurt, though we feel disorientated, we can say: "This is not our forever." One day soon, we will brawl no more with sin. One day soon Satan's vicious poison will batter us no longer. He shall lie crumpled beneath our feet. In Christ, victory is inevitable.

Part 4: Assurance (v. 14-16)

There really is no substitute for hearing it said first-hand. It just wouldn't be the same if I told one of my children: "Go tell Mammy I love her". She would much rather hear straight from my lips: "I love you". Thus far, the Psalmist has been speaking on God's behalf. Now God takes the microphone. He personally signs and seals the promises made. Repeatedly he says, "I will" as he personally drives the promises home to troubled hearts. Know for sure that the refuge offered is genuine. There is no wishful thinking here.

16: Known

"Because he holds fast to me in love, I will deliver him;
I will protect him, because he knows my name."
(Psalm 91:14)

It is all about who you know.

Safety is usually felt in the context of relationship. There is
security in the Father who is on the other end of the phone
when you need advice. There is a sense of protection in the
group of friends you have known since childhood who have got
your back. There is assurance when you know the boss is on your
side as the current project threatens to implode.

We can look for our sense of security in knowing the right
people, having the right connections or being in the right circles.
I am an introvert by temperament. I have also wrestled since
childhood with some form of social anxiety. As a result, I have
frequently felt on the isolated outside. I have a natural tendency
to assume I do not know the right people or move in the right
circles. I feel vulnerable because it is all about who you know.

This final section of the psalm radiates personal warmth from
every syllable. It pulsates with intimacy. In a rare occurrence
in the Psalms, God speaks directly to massage these promises
deep into the heart. The repeated "I will" creates a tone of
personal assurance.

Though this king walks through a fevered furnace of hardships,
the Almighty assures, *"I will deliver him"* (v. 14). The Lord
will hoist him high beyond the claws of evil. *"I will protect*

him" literally reads "I will set him up high". The Most High personally signs this pledge of preservation.

The promises of rescue and protection come in the context of intimate relationship. The one God speaks to with such tender assurance is the one who *"holds fast to me in love"* (v. 14). Moses uses the same phrase to describe God's committed love to his people: *"the LORD set his love on you"* (Deuteronomy 7:7). The singer has bound himself to the Almighty, in deep loving covenant loyalty.

Their intimacy knows chasmic depths *"he knows my name"* (v. 14). This is no mere ability to recall a collection of letters. God's name is a summary of all he is eternally. To know him is to enjoy deep and familiar intimacy. 'Know' is used elsewhere of the intimate depths of marriage. He knows the Most High with profound depth. He is not ashamed to be named as his.

Who clings to the Lord with such depth? Answering honestly, I must admit that whilst I cling to the Lord, my love is flabby and my grasp is feeble. Yes, I know the Lord, yet I often forget him or blush to be acknowledged as his. If we're hunting for assurance in how tight we cling or how deep we know, our confidence will be as steady as the Atlantic Ocean in a gale.

Switch off selfie-mode and look outward. We see Christ. He clings unyieldingly to the Father in love: *"I do as the Father has commanded me, so that the world may know that I love the Father."* (John 14:31). He knows the Father with fathomless intimacy: *"the Father knows me and I know the Father"* (John 10:15). He is the Son who has eternally known and enjoyed the Father. The

Father who delights in him has delivered and protected him. He now stands risen from the dead and ascended to the Father's right hand.

Does that leave us sitting outside gawking enviously in the window at their perfect relationship? No! One with Christ, he ushers us in to share in the warm depths of their intimacy: *"I know my own and my own know me, just as the Father knows me and I know the Father"* (John 10:14-15). We are welcomed into the inner ring, assured of the Almighty's deliverance, guaranteed the protection of the Most High.

We fear being left out. When you blend my introverted temperament with the fact that I have never lived more than four years in one place since I left home, you get a social circle more compact than most. I often feel disconnected. Sometimes friendships evaporate due to our Christian convictions. Sometimes in the furnace of grief or affliction 'friends' distance themselves or drift away with busyness. Our relational lacks leave us feeling vulnerable.

Yet it really is about who you know. If you know Christ – or should I say, are known by him – you are already in the inner ring. In Christ, we are welcomed into the intimate depths of the relationship at the heart of the universe. We are ushered into the warm kinship of the Triune God where we find deliverance and protection that infinitely surpass all the sticking-plaster solutions our world advertises. It is all about who you know.

17: Heard

"When he calls to me, I will answer him"
(Psalm 91:15)

After our eldest son was born, we arrived home from the hospital to find that the water from our taps tasted like a swimming pool. The local water treatment plant had accidentally sloshed a lot of chlorine into the local water supply making it dangerous to drink or wash in; not ideal conditions when you want to give your newborn son a bath. I got on the phone to the water supply helpline, playing the 'newborn baby' card for a bit of sympathy. "Sorry to hear that, sir. We will pass this on to a manager and get things sorted for you."

Some of the most frustrating moments in life are spent on the phone to customer support. Over the next month, I got sucked into a customer support whirlpool. Every few days, I would ring up the water company, explain our situation and ask for an update. I would be assured that someone would ring us back. When I explained that this was the fifth time I had had this exact conversation and nobody had yet called back, I was given sincere assurances that it would be different this time. Nobody ever did call back. It is a frustratingly powerless feeling to be ignored.

There are far worse situations to mine. You may be reading as a victim of abuse whose anguish is intensified by the suspicion that nobody believes your story. You may be the victim of injustice whose case has not been taken seriously because of your address or ethnicity. You may be a sufferer of chronic anxiety who feels no friend wants to hear your struggles.

When trouble finds our address, sometimes it is not the trouble itself that pains us. Sometimes it is the sensation that nobody is listening. We feel snared in numbing isolation. This can slosh over into our relationship with God, as we wonder if heaven has put our call on hold. When you think of it, what right do I, a sin-sullied creature, have to demand the attention of the infinitely holy Creator?

The warm sunshine of God's personal assurance radiates through the final lines of this Psalm. God signs the symphony of promises with a pledge: "I will". The one who has made the Almighty his refuge, need never wonder if anyone is listening. This storm-tossed singer is assured by God, "I will hear".

Thrashed by affliction, the King calls out to God, an expression of faith (*"When he calls to me..."*). So it would be with Christ. Think of his harrowed cries in Gethsemane as the horror of the cross hung before him. *"In the days of his flesh, Jesus offered up prayers and supplications, with loud cries and tears, to him who was able to save him from death"* (Hebrews 5:7).

As his cries ascend, they are not put on hold. He will not be told, "All our operators are busy right now, please try again later". He enjoys the intimately warm assurance that the Father hears. His Father will act. When *"Jesus offered up prayers and supplications, with loud cries and tears… he was heard because of his reverence"* (Hebrews 5:7). His pleas were answered. The emptied tomb is the tangible proof he was not ignored.

When we cry out as Christian believers, we do not pray nakedly. We approach the Father clothed in Christ, enveloped in his righteous robes. When we draw near to him, wounded by our sin, bruised by our circumstances, injured by others, we come as Christ's own flesh and blood. To turn us away, the Father would have to turn Christ away. To ignore our pleas, the Father would have to ignore Christ. One with him, we share the same assurance as he does. We will be heard. We will be answered.

This does not mean prayer works like a heavenly Amazon checkout. No, he loves us far too much for that. Sometimes we must wait… and wait. Sometimes the answer comes in a different size and colour. Yet in this, he is doing a work in us that is far more wonderful than simply ladling out pre-packaged replies. In the unexpected, in the waiting, he is shaping us in the image of Christ and giving us the very things we would ask for if we only truly knew what was best for us. One thing is certain though, he will never ignore our cries. He will answer.

You may feel lost in the anguish of the abuse you have suffered. You may feel trapped in the face of injustice because of your background. You may feel forgotten and floundering with chronic anxiety. Others may have put you on hold. They may have requested you try again later. He will not. He will never turn away his children. He will never dismiss their pleas. You can be sure of this: *"I will answer."*

18: Present

"I will be with him in trouble"
(Psalm 91:15)

Affliction and isolation are intimate companions. The dreary cave of depression is lonely. For all we appreciate friends walking with us through the gloom, the unrelenting darkness forces us to feel alone. In the disorientating grotto of the hospital bed, we feel unhappily secluded. For all we are grateful for the visits during the day, trying to sleep through the beeps and the bustle reminds us how far we are from the security of home. The numb cavern of grief is solitary. The surreal blur of funeral preparations have subsided, and the visits dry up as normal life resumes for all around us. But for us there is no normal to go back to. Whatever wind of trouble batters us, it usually leaves a profound sense of isolation.

A common temptation in affliction is to read our circumstances as the barometer of God's nearness. The seasons I have been submerged in the chaotic waves of mild depression have been frequently accompanied by an intense sense of abandonment. It feels like God has forgotten me. Therefore, in my isolation I need the written word of God standing outside of me in black and white. It is only when I put on the lenses of Scripture that I can correctly interpret my circumstances.

The singer of Psalm 91 is pummelled by adversity. Yet, as the waves of hardship assault him and circumstances appear to plot his downfall, the Lord seizes the microphone with words of warm tenderness: *"I will be with him in trouble"* (v.15). These words are the spectacles that reinterpret his circumstances.

To this assaulted man, the Almighty gives *himself*. No greater gift could he give. C.S. Lewis once quoted an unknown author who said: "He who has God and everything else has no more than he who has God only." [9] Moses recognised this when he prayed, *"If your presence will not go with me, do not bring us up from here"* (Exodus 33:15). Having the bounty of the promised land without God's presence is no better than the slow death of the stifling desert. To have the Most High is to lack nothing.

Jesus is *the* man pummelled by adversity, the man of sorrows. Yet he walked with assurance: *"he who sent me is with me. He has not left me alone"* (John 8:29). As Son, he has enjoyed eternal intimacy with the Father. In becoming man, he cast none of that aside.

Then we hear his desolate cry from the shadows of the cross: "I am forsaken": the moment of his deepest adversity. Here we stand before the fathomless depths of marvellous mystery. Even here, he is always with the Father, the Trinity cannot be broken. God cannot cease to be the Father loving his Son in the Spirit. Yet simultaneously, the One who is God, truly experiences God-forsakenness, plunged into blackness under the weight of our sin. He cried out "I am forsaken" so that none of those united to him would ever cry those desolate words. He bore our God-forsakenness so that, one with him, we would eternally share in his assurance of God ever present.

---

[9] Edward T. Welch, *Running Scared* (New Growth Press, 2007), 236.

Affliction is a murky cave. In Christ, a lantern is lit for us in the gloom: *"I will be with you in trouble."* In him, these words are ours. They are the lenses through which we can see our circumstances clearly. In the dismal cave of depression, we realise we are not abandoned to the blackness. The claustrophobic grotto of surgical ward 3 is filled with the blaze of his nearness. The solitary cavern of grief is not so solitary as we assumed. We are one with Christ, his own body. For God to walk out on us, he would have to walk out on Christ. His presence is that sure.

Sometimes it is only when everything is lost, we realise that *"I am with you"* is all we need. Do not let your circumstances do the exegetical work on God's faithfulness. Keep the clear lenses of the promises before your eyes. Only then will we find real assurance that the breakers of trouble will never drive you from the one who is Immanuel, God with us. As the old hymn reminds us:

> *The soul that on Jesus hath leaned for repose,*
> *I will not, I will not desert to his foes;*
> *That soul though all hell should endeavour to shake,*
> *I'll never no, never, no, never forsake!* [10]

---

[10] John Rippon, *How Firm a Foundation* (1787).

19: Honour

"I will rescue him and honour him."
(Psalm 91:15)

Humiliation is one of the forgotten side effects of suffering. The brokenness we experience can be degrading. The invasive medical procedure tears away our dignity. Our disability leaves us with the reoccurring embarrassment of being treated like a child. Our struggle with OCD makes us feel mortified even leaving the house.

Sharing in Christ's suffering can feel humiliating. Our family treat our faith in Christ as the embarrassing unmentionable. Our colleagues make snide comments as we arrive in work. Our national media subtly belittle us. Meanwhile our brothers and sisters in Christ across the globe face degrading attacks and undignified death.

There is none who knows humiliation more intensely than Christ. Our head is the One who emptied himself by taking the form of a servant, who was born into a lowly family with an address that most were ashamed of, who tasted the bitter tang of betrayal and abandonment from his closest companions, the One who experienced the shame of the cross.

Humiliation offers to write our story for us. However, the Most High speaks with tender assurance to the humiliated King that humiliation is not the last instalment in his story: *"I will rescue him and honour him"* (Psalm 91:15).

The word of the Lord reaches down into the sludgy mire: *"I will rescue him"*. He shall be hauled out of the oozing slough. No humiliation is deeper than Christ's. He was plunged into the miry depths of death, sunk to the bottom under the weight of the curse. But humiliation is not the last to speak. The Father has drawn him out of the pit of destruction, and set his feet on stable rock. He has risen. He has ascended.

Hoisted from the muck, shame and humiliation shall be reversed: *"I will honour him."* That word 'honour' is drawn from the same Hebrew root as 'glory'. He shall be glorified. He shall be exalted. The name once muttered with scorn shall be revered with eternal renown. Christ, who willingly plunged himself into the deep mire of an accursed death, now sits in the seat of supreme honour at the Father's right hand. The author to the Hebrews puts it like this, Jesus was *"crowned with glory and honour because of the suffering of death"* (Hebrews 2:9). The humiliation of Calvary was the pathway to glory.

We crave more recognition and respect. However, we cannot run from the reality that the brokenness of this world that humiliates us comes as a result of human sin. Adam's sin, in which we all share, plunged us all into the degrading depths of sin and its consequences. Jesus was without the least blotch of sin. We cannot make that claim. He alone deserves honour.

Here is the marvel of the gospel. If you are a Christian believer, Christ has taken you to himself. We are one flesh with him. With delight he says, "all that I am I give to you, and all that

_____

[11] The Church of England, *Marriage* (Church House Publishing, 2000), 7.

I have I share with you".[11] He takes our guilt and shame upon himself that we might share in his glory. In him, our story is rewritten. Humiliation is not the final page. It is now the gateway to glory.

In this broken world, humiliation will still stalk us. What is more, as Christians, humiliation will be intensified as we share in Christ's sufferings. Yet none of this can evaporate what is really real. True reality is this: we are joined to the One who sits in the seat of highest honour. One day, we shall share in his honour in all its tangible glory.

When the routines of Surgical Ward 3 have ransacked our dignity, when we feel others are talking to the wheelchair and not to us, when the frailty of old age humiliates us, remember Jesus. When shame offers to write your script, be assured that your story has already been written in Christ. The cross is the doorway to the crown.

When family shun you for your allegiance to Christ, when friends become cold, when we are marginalised for our "oppressive views", remember Jesus. When humiliation proposes to write the plot of your life, know that Christ shares his story with us. The cross is the doorway to the crown.

Humiliation will stalk us in this life. The brokenness of this world guarantees it. The hostility of this world to Christ makes sure of it. Yet, know this: humiliation is not the final chapter. We are one with Christ and a day is coming when we shall join him in glory. Shame shall dissolve as we are hoisted from the miry depths of death to reign with him.

20: Life

"With long life I will satisfy him
and show him my salvation."
(Psalm 91:16)

One fear casts its shadow over all our hardships. It troubles our troubles. Even in sunny seasons its gloom is not far away. Nobody is immune.

The fear of death is perhaps the great trouble behind all of our troubles. It loiters as the medical consultant breaks the news to us. It circles overhead as yet another job application fails. It haunts us; the anxieties flit about in our minds as we try to fall asleep.

The terror of death is a prison warden who delights to keep us captive. We are *"those who through fear of death were subject to lifelong slavery"* (Hebrews 2:15). Since Adam sinned, this tyrant has woven his chains about us. Anxiety over how we might die, fear of what lurks beyond death, dread of judgement; they can paralyse us. Our world hangs under the curse of Genesis 3. Life is cut short and death reigns. Like the vapour of our breath on a frosty morning, life is fleeting.

In a world where the shadow of death hovers relentlessly, the singer of Psalm 91 has taken refuge in the One who is life. Therefore, the melodic symphony of promises that weave through this Psalm are death-proof. He is assured of life: *"With long life I will satisfy him"* (v.16).

Length of days is an image of enjoying the blessings of the covenant. This only comes when we are united with the One who is life: *"he is your life and length of days"* (Deuteronomy 30:20). When the church father Augustine meditated on this Psalm, he saw in these words a signpost to something far greater than living into your 90's. He said, "[t]hat length is one that hath no end, eternal life, that is promised us in long days." [12] Here is a reversal of the curse we all plunged into in Adam.

Eternal length of days is much more than a continuous span of years. This is life filled with the richest of enjoyments. Under the wings of the Author of life, he looks forward to savouring all the blessings of the covenant. As the Almighty promises to *"show him my salvation"*, he is assuring him of the enjoyment of every blessing. He shall see, taste and touch salvation in all its unspeakable fullness. He shall savour life to the full.

This life is a gift fit for the King. Earlier in the Psalms, we hear this about the king: *"He asked life of you; you gave it to him, length of days forever and ever"* (Psalm 27:4). When the Lord made his covenant with David, he assured him that one of his descendants would reign forever. As the angel announced "he has risen" to two bewildered women at dawn, he was proclaiming Jesus to be this King. He has been hauled out of the abyss of death to enjoy life to the full. He now sits enthroned, enjoying all the blessings of the covenant.

When we lift our eyes to Christ, we gaze at God's salvation. In him, we hear the Almighty say to us: *"I will… show him my*

---

[12] Augustine, 'Expositions on the Book of Psalms' in Philip Schaff (ed), *The Complete Ante-Nicene & Nicene and Post Nicene Fathers Collection* Kindle Edition (Catholic Way, 2014), location 334957.

salvation." Godly old Simeon rejoiced in this, saying: *"Lord, now you are letting your servant depart in peace… for my eyes have seen your salvation"* (Luke 2:29-30).

We live in a world held captive by death's terrors. However, the moment Christ took hold of us, the prison doors were unbolted. One with him, we share his life. Death has lost its grip on us. Whether we are anxious over how we might die, or we are fearful of what loiters beyond death, or we are paralysed by dread of judgement, we look to Christ. To see Jesus is to see God's salvation. As believers, we have already died and risen in him, the resurrection day is a mere formality. His present experience is our assured future. We shall rise to savour life to the full.

However hard the waves of adversity thrash us, however loud the gales of trouble bellow, however dark the shadows that engulf us, they cannot steal our life. Christ is our life. He is risen and ascended, and because we are one with him, so shall we. The dawn is coming. We shall soon wake on the morning of resurrection day. On that day, we shall see the One who is God's salvation face to face. On that day, we shall savour life in all its fullness. No more Kleenex. No more hospitals. No more funerals.

However long your life in this world is to be, however deep the mire you are trudging through right now, however dark the shadow that submerges you, if you are Christ's then these words are yours: *"With long life I will satisfy you and show you my salvation"*.

21: In the Shadow of the Almighty

*"He who dwells in the shelter of the Most High
will abide in the shadow of the Almighty."*
(Psalm 91:1)

On the 8th of January 1956, 28 year old Jim Elliot was speared
to death, alongside four others on a sandbar in Ecuador's
Curaray river.[13] Jim, Nate, Ed, Peter, and Roger were seeking to
reach the Huaorani (or "Auca") Indians, for the first time with
the gospel. Waiting back at base camp was his wife Elizabeth
and their 10-month-old daughter. Later, when Elizabeth
published her husband's story, she called the book *Shadow of the
Almighty*, deliberately recalling the opening verse of Psalm 91.[14]

Elizabeth Elliot recognised that living under the shadow of the
Almighty does not immunise us against pain. The shelter of the
Most High does not shield us from sorrow, suffering or even the
most brutal death. Consider Christ, the singer of the Psalm. He
always enjoyed the refuge of the shadow of the Almighty. Yet, he
is also called *"a man of sorrows and acquainted with grief"* (Isaiah
53:3). He has felt the knocks of rejection, grief and betrayal. He
knows what it is to be beaten, mocked and hung in shame to
die. The shadow of the Almighty did not snatch him away from
the shadow of the cross.

---

[13] John Piper, *'Slain in the Shadow of the Almighty'* (Desiring God, 2016). Online at: https://www.
desiringgod.org/articles/slain-in-the-shadow-of-the-almighty

[14] I am indebted to Christopher Ash for this illustration. Christopher Ash, *Psalms For
You* (The Good Book Company, 2020), 186.

United to him, we cannot expect any different. Christian believers are battered by illness and money troubles, we are assaulted by anxiety and chronic pain, we may face mental illness, abuse, disability, rejection, sneers and even violent death. The shadow of the Almighty does not remove the shadow of the cross.

However, by choosing to call a book about her martyred husband *Shadow of the Almighty*, Elizabeth Elliot was saying something magnificent about the treasury of promises found in this Psalm. If we are under the protecting shade of the Most High, nothing we face in life or death can abolish the security we have in Christ. We may not be sheltered *from* the tempest trouble in this life, but we will be sheltered *through* every trouble, shielded for something more glorious.

These promises offer enduring hope. They offer the hope of resurrection. Consider Christ, the King to whom these promises are made. He now savours all this Psalm points to. He was not sheltered from the cross, but he has been sheltered through the cross. He is risen. He has ascended. He now revels in infinite delight at the Father's right hand.

Yet, he is also waiting. He is waiting for the day his body, the church, joins him. As a bride is one flesh with her husband, as the branches are connected to the vine, as the body is connected to the head, so we are one with Christ. All that is his is now ours. The rich storehouse of promises in this Psalm are unlocked and dished out to us in Christ without restraint. His present experience is our assured future. The hour is coming when the shadowy gloom of this life will be scattered by the radiant dawn of resurrection morning, and the bride shall run into the arms of her groom.

Whatever wind of trouble prompted you to take up this book, be sure of one thing as you put it down: If you are in Christ, nothing in this life can touch your eternal security. In this life, we may be thrashed by abuse or Alzheimer's, by bullying or bankruptcy, by cancer or car crashes, by depression or death. Yet, none of these things have any power to snatch us out from under the shadow of the Almighty. We rest under his shelter, and this shepherd will lose none of his sheep. We are as secure as Christ is.

Wherever the gusts of trouble seem to be blowing you, never forget where you are. In Christ, you dwell in the shelter of the Most High, under the shadow of the Almighty. This means our future is secure. After all if he who did not spare his own Son but gave him up for us all, *"how will he not also with him graciously give us all things?"* (Romans 8:32).

Epilogue

Where do we go from here?

Sometimes I find myself picking up a book, naively hoping that by the time I have turned over the last page, the problem that prompted my to pick it up has evaporated. It never does. Though we have come to the end of this little book, trouble is not finished barging into our lives. Jesus promises his followers: *"In the world you will have tribulation"* (John 16:33). Until Christ returns trouble will keep on troubling us.

Where do we go from here?

Perhaps the most important thing you can do as you put down this book is to keep meditating on the promises of God. Cultivating a habit of chewing over the Bible will give us a rooted stability when the winds of trouble buffet us. Essentially, this book has been a tool to help you meditate on God's word so that you might sink your roots deeper into him.

The first time I stepped up to the pulpit in the chapel in theological college, I noticed a little brass plaque. It is a permanent Post-It note to any preacher before they open their mouth. Engraved on it are words from John 12, when a cluster of Greeks come looking to meet Jesus. They say to Philip: *"Sir, we would see Jesus"* (John 12:21 KJV). The plaque's message is simple: "As you stand to preach, what we need most is to see Christ."

As you open your Bible, let that be your prayer: "Show me Christ". In the blaze of affliction what we need most is not motivational quotes, clever hacks or even good advice.

We need Christ. In him alone we find the refuge our weary souls crave. It is in the Bible we encounter him. Biblical meditation is the habit of not closing our Bibles until we have seen him and enjoyed his beauty.

Can I let you in on a secret before we finish? The chapters you have just read have been a subtle training exercise. As I have written, I have tried to model how to meditate on God's word in such a way that we do not leave without seeing Christ. Each chapter follows the same basic pattern. Before I leave you, allow me show you my workings. In each meditation I have asked the same three questions:

1. **What is being sung?** What is being said in this Psalm? Pick one theme to focus on.

2. **How does Christ sing this?** How does this Psalm show me Christ? Think of one episode from the Gospels that illustrates this.

3. **How do we sing this in Christ?** What are the implications for those who are one with Christ? Pick one particular area of your life right now where this will make a difference.

I offer these questions to you as a simple toolkit that you can take away to help you cultivate a habit of meditating on God's word. You do not need to spend hours doing this. If you can only focus for a few minutes in the blizzard, that is OK. The important thing is that you keep looking to Christ, whatever capacity you have right now. Only by prayerfully pondering God's word will we find rooted stability for the gales of hardship. At the pulsating heart of that word is Christ, our refuge. So keep going. Keep opening your Bible and calling out: "Show me Christ!"

As a next step, why not choose another Psalm and use these three questions to work your way through it at your own pace. I have found that a pen and paper helps my restless mind focus longer. If you want a little more help with meditating on the Bible, I recommend Linda Allcock's fantastic book *Deeper Still*. [15]

So… where do we go from here? We go to Christ. Day after day, we go back to him. Day after day, we open our Bibles pleading "we would see Jesus".

We go to Christ. Where else can we go? In him alone, our life is hidden and secure. In him alone is refuge.

---

[15] Linda Allcock, *Deeper Still: Finding Clear Minds and Full Hearts through Biblical Meditation* (The Good Book Company, 2020).